92 Fertility Enhancing Meal and Juice Recipes:

Become More Fertile Faster

By

Joe Correa CSN

COPYRIGHT

© 2019 Live Stronger Faster Inc.

All rights reserved

Reproduction or translation of any part of this work beyond that permitted by section 107 or 108 of the 1976 United States Copyright Act without the permission of the copyright owner is unlawful.

This publication is designed to provide accurate and authoritative information in regard to the subject matter covered. It is sold with the understanding that neither the author nor the publisher is engaged in rendering medical advice. If medical advice or assistance is needed, consult with a doctor. This book is considered a guide and should not be used in any way detrimental to your health. Consult with a physician before starting this nutritional plan to make sure it's right for you.

ACKNOWLEDGEMENTS

This book is dedicated to my friends and family that have had mild or serious illnesses so that you may find a solution and make the necessary changes in your life.

92 Fertility Enhancing Meal and Juice Recipes:

Become More Fertile Faster

By

Joe Correa CSN

CONTENTS

Copyright

Acknowledgements

About The Author

Introduction

Commitment

92 Fertility Enhancing Meal and Juice Recipes: Become More Fertile Faster

Additional Titles from This Author

ABOUT THE AUTHOR

After years of Research, I honestly believe in the positive effects that proper nutrition can have over the body and mind. My knowledge and experience has helped me live healthier throughout the years and which I have shared with family and friends. The more you know about eating and drinking healthier, the sooner you will want to change your life and eating habits.

Nutrition is a key part in the process of being healthy and living longer so get started today. The first step is the most important and the most significant.

INTRODUCTION

92 Fertility Enhancing Meal and Juice Recipes: Become More Fertile Faster

By Joe Correa CSN

This book is a collection of recipes based on healthy foods that will provide all the necessary nutrients in order to increase fertility and to help your body get back to its hormonal balance, which is an extremely important aspect of fertility.

Reproduction is a common thing for all living beings. However, sometimes it doesn't happen at the moment when we plan it. When you dig just a little bit under the surface, you'll find out that difficulties with conceiving are occurring more often then it seems. And it happens all over the world.

Taking care of your reproductive health and preparing for pregnancy mean that you'll have to change some of your habits, especially eating habits.

Various studies have shown that a healthy diet can improve and boost fertility. It can also prevent recurrent miscarriages, support pregnancy, and increase overall health in a new mother. A meal packed with different nutrients is the key to a healthy reproductive system – both sperm and eggs are literally protected with antioxidants, vitamins, and minerals.

My recipes are based on foods that will help your body maintain its hormonal balance by increasing nutrient intake to give you the chance to have a normal and healthy pregnancy.

Another important issue I would like to mention is that all of these recipes are based on organic foods. You should always keep that in mind when preparing these meals. Pesticides and herbicides in conventional food production are harmful and they have negative effects fertility in both men and women. Always chose organic fruits and vegetables that are not only free of different chemicals but also have a lot more nutrients than processed foods.

Saturated fats, cholesterol, and essential fatty acids are important for the development of a fetus and its growth. Foods like fish, coconut oil, grass-fed meats, nuts, seeds, and so on, are enriched with healthy cholesterol that will maintain hormone production in your body. This book will teach you how to prepare these delicious meals without much effort.

Taking care of your health before and during pregnancy means that you are creating a new and healthy life for your future child.

COMMITMENT

In order to improve my condition, I *(your name)*, commit to eating more of these foods on a daily basis and to exercise at least 30 minutes daily:

- Berries (especially blueberries), peaches, cherries, apples, apricots, oranges, lemon juice, grapefruit, tangerines, mandarins, pears, etc.
- Broccoli, spinach, collard greens, sweet potatoes, avocado, artichoke, baby corn, carrots, celery, cauliflower, onions, etc.
- Whole grains, steel-cut oats, oatmeal, quinoa, barley, etc.
- Black beans, red bean beans, garbanzo beans, lentils, etc.
- Nuts and seeds including: walnuts, cashews, flaxseeds, sesame seeds, etc.
- Fish
- 8 – 10 glasses of water

Sign here

X_____

92 FERTILITY ENHANCING MEAL AND JUICE RECIPES: BECOME MORE FERTILE FASTER

MEAL RECIPES

1. Fresh Apple Juice Smoothie

Ingredients:

1 cup of baby spinach, chopped

½ cup of English cucumber, peeled and sliced

¼ cup of apple juice, unsweetened

¼ cup of fresh water

Preparation:

Combine all ingredients in a blender. Blend until smooth mixture. Transfer the mixture to a serving glasses. Refrigerate for about 20 minutes before serving.

Nutrition information per serving: Kcal: 110, Protein: 4.5g, Carbs: 22.1g, Fats: 1.5g

2. Salmon and Asparagus Omelet

Ingredients:

4 oz of wild salmon slices, dried

8 free-range eggs

¼ cup of onion, diced

3 oz of asparagus, cooked

1 tbsp of milk, organic

2 tsp of canola oil

1 garlic clove, diced

2 tbsp of fresh parsley, finely chopped

1 tsp of lemon juice

1 tsp of chives, minced

1 tsp of fresh dill, minced

Preparation:

Preheat the oil in a nonstick frying pan over a medium-high temperature. Add the onion and stir-fry for 1 minute, then add asparagus continue to cook for another minute. Stir in the lemon juice and spread the vegetables evenly on the bottom.

Combine eggs, milk and spices in a large mixing bowl. Season with some salt and pepper to taste. Pour in the egg mixture to the pan and cook for 1 minute.

Stir in the egg mixture and top with salmon slices. Reduce the heat to low and cook for 3 minutes more, or until eggs are set. Remove from the heat and use a spatula to fold the omelet before serving.

Nutrition information per serving: Kcal: 350, Protein: 40.5g, Carbs: 9.7g, Fats: 14.2g

3. Cucumber & Apple Smoothie

Ingredients:

½ cup of apple juice, unsweetened

½ medium-sized cucumber, peeled and sliced

½ cup of spinach, chopped

½ cup of water

1tsp of hemp seed

Preparation:

Place all ingredients in a blender or a food processor. Blend until smooth and transfer to a serving glasses. Serve with some ice cubes before serving.

Nutrition information per serving: Kcal: 198, Protein: 6.1g, Carbs: 30.6g, Fats: 6.3g

4. Mackerel with Garlic

Ingredients:

1 lb of mackerel, whole, cleaned

15 garlic cloves, crushed

4 large carrots, sliced

2 tbsp of olive oil

3 medium-sized zucchinis, sliced

1 tsp of salt

1 tsp of black pepper, ground

Preparation:

Preheat the oven to 400°F.

Rub the salt and pepper into the fish. Take a large baking sheet and grease it with oil. Spread crushed garlic onto the bottom of the sheet. Place the fishes onto it and put it in the oven. Bake for about 25 minutes.

Meanwhile, combine vegetables in a pot of boiling water and cook for 2-3 minutes, or until fork-tender. remove from the heat and season with salt and pepper to taste.

When all done, serve the fish and vegetables. For extra

flavor, add a few lemon wedges.

Nutrition information per serving: Kcal: 710, Protein: 27.5g, Carbs: 10.5g, Fats: 56.2g

5. Warm Garden Salad

Ingredients:

3 medium-sized zucchinis, peeled and shredded

1 medium-sized yellow squash, peeled and shredded

2 garlic clove, minced

1 large carrot, shredded

1 tbsp of honey

2 tbsp of lemon juice

1 tsp of salt

1 tsp of black pepper, ground

Preparation:

Preheat the oil in a large skillet over a medium-high temperature. add the onion and garlic and stir-fry until translucent. Now, add all other ingredients and season with salt and pepper to taste. Cook for 10 minutes or until tender. Serve warm.

Nutrition information per serving: Kcal: 710, Protein: 27.5g, Carbs: 10.5g, Fats: 56.2g

6. Fresh Cliantro Chicken

Ingredients:

6 chicken pieces (legs and breasts), skinless

2 tsp of vegetable oil

2 cups of long grain rice

4 cups of water

2 medium-sized tomatoes, chopped

1 medium-sized green pepper, chopped

1 medium-sized red pepper, chopped

2 garlic cloves, minced

1 medium-sized carrot

4 cups of corn, frozen

2 oz of black olives

½ cup of celery, finely chopped

1 medium-sized onion

1 tbsp of fresh cilantro, finely chopped

¼ tsp of salt

¼ tsp of black pepper, ground

2 cloves garlic, chopped fine

Preparation:

Preheat the oil in a deep pot over a medium-high temperature. Add chicken and cook until brown. Add all ingredients except rice and olives. Pour water enough to cover all ingredients. Cover with a lid and reduce temperature to low. Cook for 30 minutes, or until meat is done. Remove from the heat.

Meanwhile, combine rice and olives in a cooking pot. Pour water enough to cover all ingredients. Sprinkle with some salt and cover with a lid. Cook on medium temperature for about 20 minutes. remove from the heat and serve with chicken and veggies.

Nutrition information per serving: Kcal: 448, Protein: 24.5g, Carbs: 71.4g, Fats: 7.5g

7. Quinoa Blueberry Smoothie

Ingredients:

¼ cup of white quinoa, pre-cooked

½ cup of blueberries, frozen

½ cup of spinach, finely chopped

½ cup of Greek yogurt, organic

2 tbsp of skim milk, organic

Preparation:

Combine all ingredients in a food processor. Blend until smooth and transfer to a serving glasses. Refrigerate for 20 minutes before serving.

Nutrition information per serving: Kcal: 121, Protein: 7.1g, Carbs: 22.5g, Fats: 1.2g

8. Seashell Pasta

Ingredients:

1 lb pack seashell pasta

2 tbsp of vegetable oil

½ cup of apple cider vinegar

½ cup of wine vinegar

½ cup of water

3 tbsp of yellow mustard

¼ tsp of black pepper, ground

2 pimentos, sliced

2 small cucumbers, sliced

2 small onions, sliced

1 lettuce head

Preparation:

Use the package instructions to cook pasta. Drain and rinse well. Place it in a large bowl and set aside.

Combine vinegar, water, pimento, mustard, salt, and pepper. Blend until smooth. Pour the mixture over the pasta.

Add cucumber and onion slices and give it a good stir. Refrigerate overnight to allow flavors to mingle. Drain before serving and serve on lettuce leaves.

Nutrition information per serving: Kcal: 158, Protein: 4.2g, Carbs: 31.5g, Fats: 2.7g

9. Scallop Skewers

Ingredients:

3 medium-sized bell peppers, cut into bite-sized pieces

1 lb fresh bay scallops

1 cup of cherry tomatoes, halved

¼ cup of balsamic vinegar

¼ cup of vegetable oil

3 tbsp of lemon juice

½ tsp of garlic powder

¼ tsp of black pepper, ground

Skewers

Preparation:

Place bell peppers in a boiling water and cook for 2 minutes. Remove from the heat and drain.

Thread tomatoes, scallop, and then pepper on skewers. Combine all other ingredients in a mixing bowl and stir well to combine. Drizzle with marinade and place on the grill.

Grill for about 15 minutes or until set. Remove from the

grill and serve.

Nutrition information per serving: Kcal: 223, Protein: 30.4g, Carbs: 13.7g, Fats: 6.8g

10. Black Beans and Artichoke Pasta

Ingredients:

1 lb of artichoke hearts, drained and chopped

1 lb of black beans, canned, drained and rinsed

1 lb of penne pasta

1 cup of spring onions, finely chopped

2 large tomatoes, chopped

2 garlic cloves, crushed

1 tbsp of extra-virgin oil

½ tsp of salt

¼ tsp of black pepper, ground

¼ tsp of dried basil, ground

½ tsp of Cayenne pepper

Preparation:

Use the package instructions to cook pasta. Drain and transfer to a large bowl.

Place artichoke in a pot of boiling water and cook for 5 minutes. Remove from the heat and drain. Combine artichokes with pasta and set aside.

Preheat the oil in a large saucepan over a medium-high temperature. Add the onions and stir-fry for about 4-5 minutes, or until soften. Stir in tomatoes, garlic, and a pinch of salt, pepper, and basil to taste. Cover with a lid and cook for another 10 minutes. Now, add beans, cayenne pepper and reduce the heat to low. Cover with a lid and cook for 10-15 minutes, or until beans tender. Remove from the heat.

Pour the mixture over the pasta and stir well to combine. Serve immediately.

Nutrition information per serving: Kcal: 324, Protein: 16.3g, Carbs: 58.4g, Fats: 3.4g

11. Cheesy Tomato Couscous with Basil

Ingredients:

4 large tomatoes, diced

1 cup of couscous

½ cup of Mozzarella, organic, shredded

3 tbsp of shallots, minced

1 tbsp of olive oil

1 tsp of fresh lemon juice

1 garlic clove, minced

1 cup of water

¼ cup of fresh basil leaves

½ tsp of sea salt

¼ tsp of black pepper, ground

Preparation:

Combine tomato, cheese, garlic, shallots, lemon juice, and olive oil. Sprinkle with salt and pepper and stir well. Cover and refrigerate for 30 minutes to marinate.

Bring one cup of water to boil in a large skillet over a

medium-high temperature. Stir in the couscous and remove from the heat. Cover with a lid and set aside for 5 minutes to cool.

Now, combine tomato mixture and couscous in a large serving bowl. Give it a good stir and top with basil leaves. Serve.

Nutrition information per serving: Kcal: 283, Protein: 13.7g, Carbs: 7.4g, Fats: 14.3g

12. Asian Chicken Salad

Ingredients:

4 chicken breasts, cut into bite-sized pieces

1 medium-sized Romaine lettuce head

1 cup of fresh mandarin oranges, wedged

½ cup of Parmesan cheese, organic, shredded

½ cup of fresh strawberries, halved

2 tbsp of walnuts, chopped

1 cup of fresh spinach, chopped

1 tsp of balsamic vinegar

Preparation:

Place the meat chops in a nonstick frying pan. Cook the meat for 10 minutes on both sides. Remove from the heat and set aside.

Take a salad bowl or a plate and make layers in the following order: lettuce, spinach, meat, oranges, strawberries. Sprinkle with walnuts and top with shredded cheese. Drizzle with vinegar and toss well before serving.

Nutrition information per serving: Kcal: 223, Protein: 16.2g, Carbs: 9.9g, Fats: 10.3g

13. Fresh Rosemary Tuna

Ingredients:

1 lb of tuna steaks

5 tbsp of olive oil

2 tbsp of lime juice

2 tsp of cumin, ground

1 tbsp of fresh rosemary, finely chopped

2 tsp of dried cilantro, ground

Preparation:

Combine oil, lime juice, cilantro, and cumin a marinade bowl. Place the fish and coat well with marinade. Refrigerate for at least 20 minutes.

Preheat the grill to a medium-high temperature. Place the meat on a grill and reserve the marinade. Turn over the meat every 2 minutes and spoon the marinade over while grilling. Grill until charcoal edges.

Nutrition information per serving: Kcal: 230, Protein: 27.4g, Carbs: 1.2g, Fats: 17.3g

14. Cabbage and Tomato Salad

Ingredients:

1 small cabbage head, shredded

2 medium-sized tomatoes, cubed

1 cup of red cabbage, shredded

2 tbsp of fresh cilantro, chopped

¼ tsp of salt

¼ tsp of black pepper, ground

Preparation:

Combine cilantro, salt, and pepper in a small mixing bowl. Stir and set aside.

Combine cabbage, tomatoes and red cabbage in a large salad bowl. Drizzle with previously prepared spice mixture.

Serve.

Nutrition information per serving: Kcal: 43, Protein: 2.1g, Carbs: 7.9g, Fats: 1.2g

15. Turkey Soup

Ingredients:

1 lb of turkey breasts, skinless, boneless, cubed

½ cup of mushrooms

1 garlic clove, minced

1 medium-sized onion, diced

2 cups of tomato pasta

1 cup of chicken broth, low-sodium

1 cup of celery, finely chopped

1 medium-sized bell pepper, chopped

3 small potatoes, peeled and cubed

1 tsp od paprika, ground

1 cup of peas

1 tbsp of fresh parsley, finely chopped

1 tsp of dried oregano, ground

½ tsp of black pepper, ground

½ tsp of salt

Preparation:

Place the meat in a large nonstick saucepan. Sprinkle with paprika and cook for 5 minutes over a medium-high temperature. Remove the meat from a saucepan and set aside. Now, place the mushrooms, peppers, garlic, onions, and celery into the saucepan. Stir well and cook for 5 minutes. Add remaining ingredients and meat. Stir well and cover with a lid. Reduce the heat and cook for about 40 minutes, stirring occasionally.

Remove from the heat and serve warm.

Nutrition information per serving: Kcal: 278, Protein: 33.2g, Carbs: 31.7g, Fats: 4.8g

16. Tomato & Broccoli Salad

Ingredients:

3 cups of tomatoes, chopped

1 lb of broccoli, halved

1 cup of sour cream, organic, fat-free

½ cup of skim milk, organic

1 tsp of curry powder

1 tsp of dry mustard

¼ tsp of salt

5-6 Romaine lettuce leaves

Preparation:

Carefully put broccoli in a pot of boiling water. Cook for about 5 minutes or until tender. Remove from the heat and drain well. Set aside to cool.

Place tomatoes into a blender. Add a pinch of salt to taste. Blend until smooth mixture. Set aside.

Meanwhile, combine milk, sour cream, and spices. Whisk to combine and pour over the broccoli. Refrigerate for 2 hours to allow flavours to meld.

Line lettuce leaves sheets on a serving plate and spoon the salad. Top with previously made tomato puree.

Nutrition information per serving: Kcal: 109, Protein: 4.1g, Carbs: 11.2g, Fats: 1.2g

17. Red Bell Pepper Frittata

Ingredients:

2 large bell peppers, chopped

8 free-range eggs

2 tbsp of parmesan cheese, organic

1 tsp of olive oil

½ cup of fresh parsley, chopped

½ cup of fresh celery, chopped

1 small onion, chopped

2 garlic cloves, minced

¼ tsp of black pepper, ground

Preparation:

Combine eggs, parsley, and black pepper in a mixing bowl. Whisk well and set aside.

Preheat the oil in a large frying pan over a medium-high temperature. Add garlic, celery, onion and peppers. Cook for 5 minutes stirring occasionally. Pour over the egg mixture and spread evenly. Cook until eggs are set. Remove from the heat and sprinkle with cheese. Fold the omelet and serve.

Nutrition information per serving: Kcal: 340, Protein: 22.1g, Carbs: 23.1g, Fats: 15.2g

18. Mushroom and Garlic Soup

Ingredients:

1 lb of button mushrooms, chopped

1 medium-sized onion, chopped

1 cup of fresh spinach, chopped

4 cups of chicken stock, unsalted

2 tsp of vegetable oil

2 cups of water

1 cup of quinoa, pre-cooked

3 garlic cloves, minced

¼ tsp of salt

¼ tsp of black pepper, ground

1 tsp of fresh thyme, chopped

Preparation:

Preheat the oil in a large skillet on a low temperature. Add the onion and stir-fry for 5-6 minutes or until translucent. Add mushrooms, cover, with a lid and cook for 10 minutes and set aside. Now, add all garlic, quinoa, thyme, and salt.

Cook for 20 minutes more and remove from the heat. Wait few minutes to cool and transfer to a food processor. Blend and return to the skillet. Add all other remaining ingredients and cook for 10 minutes, stirring occasionally. Sprinkle with salt and pepper to taste.

Serve warm.

Nutrition information per serving: Kcal: 110, Protein: 4.2g, Carbs: 18.6g, Fats: 2.5g

19. Lima Beans with Fennel

Ingredients:

2 cups of fresh lima beans

1 cup of fennel, chopped

1 small onion, diced

½ cup of vegetable broth, unsalted

1 cup of spinach, finely chopped

1 tbsp of apple cider vinegar

1 tbsp of olive oil

¼ tsp of black pepper, ground

Preparation:

Place lima beans in a pot of boiling water and cook for about 10 minutes. Remove from the heat and drain well.

Preheat the oil in large skillet over a medium-high temperature. Add onion and fennel and cook for 5 minutes, or until tender.

Add lima beans and vegetable stock to the skillet and stir well. Cook for 2-3 minutes and then add spinach. Reduce the heat to low and cover with a lid. Cook for 10 minutes.

Remove from the heat, and stir in vinegar and pepper. Let it stand for a while and serve.

Nutrition information per serving: Kcal: 93, Protein: 5.2g, Carbs: 15.3g, Fats: 4.2g

20. Dark Chocolate Cookies

Ingredients:

¼ cup of cocoa powder, sifted

8 tbsp of butter, unsalted

1 cup of dark chocolate chips

2 large eggs

1 cup of wheat flour

1 tsp of peppermint extract

1 tbsp of honey

1 tsp of baking soda

¼ tsp of salt

Preparation:

Preheat the oven to 370°F.

Combine butter and honey in a mixing bowl. Use kitchen mixer and mix until fluffy. Add eggs and whisk until smooth. Set aside.

Combine flour, baking soda, cocoa, and salt in a separate large bowl. Mix well to combine and stir in the chocolate chips.

Now combine both previously made mixtures and squeeze with hands to get a nice dough. Shape up the balls and place in a baking sheet. Gently press the top of each ball to form the cookies.

Bake 10-12 minutes, or until lightly soft and crisp edges. Remove from the oven and place cookies on a rack to cool for a while.

Serve!

Nutrition information per serving: Kcal: 121, Protein: 2.2g, Carbs: 14.5g, Fats: 7.3g

21. Veggies and Cheese Frittata

Ingredients:

8 large eggs

½ lb of button mushrooms, sliced

½ lb of shiitake mushrooms, sliced

1 large onion, sliced

1 garlic clove, minced

1 cup of tomatoes, blended

½ cup of olives, pitted and halved

4 tbsp of milk, organic

3 tbsp of all-purpose flour

1 tsp of baking powder

1 tsp of Himalayan salt

½ tsp of black pepper, ground

Preparation:

Preheat the oven to 400°F.

Beat the eggs in a large mixing bowl. Add flour, baking

powder, and milk and stir until all combine and transform into a lumpy batter. Set aside.

Preheat the oil in a large frying pan over a medium-high temperature. Add mushrooms and onions and cook for 10 minutes, or until fork-tender. Stir in garlic and cook for about 2-3 minutes more. Pour over the blended tomatoes, and add olives. Stir again, and reduce the heat to low. Pour over the previously made batter and stir until combined with vegetables. Cook for another 3-4 minutes and remove from the heat.

Transfer all to a baking sheet and place it in the oven. Bake for 10 minutes, then reduce the heat to 350°F and bake for another 25 minutes or until slightly golden color. Remove from the heat and cut into portions. Serve warm.

Nutrition information per serving: Kcal:221, Protein: 11.5g, Carbs: 32.4g, Fats: 14.2g

22. Chicken Zucchini Pie

Ingredients:

4 oz of chicken breasts, skinless and boneless, cubed

1 medium-sized zucchini, peeled and chopped

2 medium-sized tomatoes, chopped

1 medium-sized onion, sliced

1 cup of skim milk, organic

4 large eggs

2 tbsp of cream cheese, organic

¼ tsp of black pepper, ground

Preparation:

Preheat the oven to 400°F.

Combine, meat, onion, zucchini, cheese, and tomatoes in a large bowl. Stir well to combine and transfer to a baking pie plate. Set aside.

Whisk together eggs, cheese, milk, and pepper. Pour over and spread equally over a previously made meat mixture.

Bake for 40 minutes or until a fork inserted comes out

clean. Remove from the oven and let it cool for 5 minutes. Cut into portions and serve.

Nutrition information per serving: Kcal: 156, Protein: 15.2g, Carbs: 16.2g, Fats: 5.6g

23. Spinach and Strawberry Salad

Ingredients:

1 lb of fresh baby spinach, chopped

1 lb of strawberries, halved

1 medium-sized cucumber, sliced

¼ cup of red onion, finely chopped

2 tbsp of almonds, roughly chopped

2 tbsp of lemon juice

1 tbsp of vegetable vinegar

1 tbsp of honey

¼ tsp of salt

Preparation:

Combine lemon juice, vinegar, honey, and salt in a small mixing bowl. Set aside to allow flavors to mingle.

Combine spinach, strawberries, cucumber, onion, and almonds in a large salad bowl. Toss well to combine.

Drizzle the marinade over the salad and serve!

Nutrition information per serving: Kcal: 142, Protein: 4.5g, Carbs: 20.3g, Fats: 7.5g

24. Zucchini Lasagna

Ingredients:

2 lbs of zucchinis, peeled and chopped

8 oz of ricotta cheese, organic

8 oz of Mozzarella cheese, organic, shredded

¼ cup of Parmesan cheese, organic, shredded

2 cups of homemade tomato paste

8 oz of lasagna noodles

Preparation:

Preheat the oven to 375°F.

Grease a large baking sheet with vegetable oil spray. Make the first layer out of a tomato paste. Top with 3 noodles.

Now, laxer the zucchini slices. In a separate bowl, combine ricotta, parmesan and mozzarella and use about 1/3 of the mixture for the next layer. Repeat the process until all ingredients are used.

Bake for about 40 minutes and remove from the oven. Set aside to cool and cut into serving portions.

You can also add more vegetables or change the layer's

order.

Nutrition information per serving: Kcal: 453, Protein: 23.5g, Carbs: 53.2g, Fats: 17.6g

25. Beet and Avocado Salad

Ingredients:

4 medium red beets, scrubbed, peeled, halved

1 ripe avocado, pitted, peeled, chopped

10 cherry tomatoes, halved

1 cup of organic Gala apples

1 medium-sized carrot, sliced

1 tbsp of balsamic vinegar

2 tbsp of extra-virgin olive oil

¼ tsp of Cayenne pepper

¼ tsp of black pepper, ground

¼ tsp of salt

Preparation:

Gently place the beets in a pot of boiling water. Cook for about 15 minutes, or until fork-tender.

Combine oil, vinegar and cayenne pepper. Add a pinch of salt and pepper to taste and stir well. Set aside.

Combine avocado chops, apple, carrot, tomatoes , carrot,

and cashews in a large salad bowl. Stir in the beets and drizzle all with dressing. Once again, give it a good stir and serve.

Nutrition information per serving: Kcal: 191, Protein: 4.2g, Carbs: 5.3g, Fats: 17.3g

26. Baked Salmon with Mustard

Ingredients:

1 lb of salmon fillet,

1 cup of sour cream, organic

2 tbsp of Dijon mustard

3 tbsp of fresh scallions, finely chopped

2 tsp of dried dill, ground

2 tbsp of lemon juice

1 garlic clove, minced

¼ tsp of black pepper, ground

1 tsp of grapeseed oil

Preparation:

Preheat the oven to 400°F.

Combine mustard, lemon juice, sour cream, scallions and dill in a mixing bowl. Set aside to allow flavors meld.

Grease a large baking sheet and place the meat. Add garlic and sprinkle with some pepper to taste. Pour over the previously made sauce.

Bake for about 20 minutes. Serve with some fresh vegetables.

Nutrition information per serving: Kcal: 196, Protein: 27.3g, Carbs: 5.4g, Fats: 7.3g

27. Green Beans with Cheddar Cheese

Ingredients:

1 lb of fresh green beans, cut into bite-sized pieces

1 large onion, sliced

2 oz of cheddar cheese, organic, crumbled

½ tsp of salt

¼ tsp of black pepper, ground

1 tbsp of fresh parsley, finely chopped

Preparation:

Gently place beans into a pot of boiling water. Cook for about 10 minutes or until fork-tender. remove from the heat and drain well.

Preheat the oil in a large frying pan and add onions. Stir-fry until translucent. Add green beans and sprinkle with some salt and pepper to taste. Cook for about 3-4 minutes and remove from the heat. Top with cheese and fresh parsley.

Nutrition information per serving: Kcal: 164, Protein: 9.4g, Carbs: 8.2g, Fats: 13.4g

28. Orange Banana Smoothie

Ingredients:

2 medium-sized oranges, peeled and wedged

1 medium-sized banana, sliced

½ cup of Greek yogurt, organic

1 tbsp of honey

1 tbsp of cinnamon, ground

Preparation:

Combine all ingredients in a blender. Blend until smooth and transfer to a serving glasses. Add few ice cubes and enjoy!

Nutrition information per serving: Kcal: 164, Protein: 2.3g, Carbs: 40.4g, Fats: 0.8g

29. Chicken Creole with Mango

Ingredients:

1 lb of chicken breasts, skinless and boneless

1 medium-sized carrot, sliced

2 mangoes, peeled, pitted and chopped

2 medium-sized bell peppers, chopped

2 tbsp of homemade tomato paste

2 tbsp of cornstarch

1 small onion, sliced

3 tbsp of balsamic vinegar

1 cup of orange juice

½ cup of lime juice

1 garlic clove, crushed

¼ tsp of salt

¼ tsp of black pepper, ground

2 tbsp of water

Preparation:

Combine lime juice, orange juice, garlic, and pepper in a marinade bowl. Place the meat and coat well with marinade. Cover and set aside for 1 hour, coating occasionally.

Transfer the meat to a large frying pan and add bell peppers. Pour enough water to cover all ingredients and bring to a boil. Remove the meat and reserve the pan. Pat dry the meat.

Add onion, vinegar and tomato paste to the skillet. Cook for 2 minutes over a medium temperature.

In a separate bowl. Combine cornstarch and water, stir well and add it to the pan. Stir all well to combine and cook until thickens. Reduce the heat to low and add mango chops. Cook one minute and remove from the heat.

Place the chicken on a serving plate and spoon the sauce over. Top with some fresh parsley or dried oregano sprinkle. This is, however, optional.

Nutrition information per serving: Kcal: 283, Protein: 19.4g, Carbs: 43.2g, Fats: 5.5g

30. Feta and Olive Meatballs

Ingredients:

1 lb ground lamb meat, (grass-fed)

½ cup of olives, pitted

½ cup of Feta cheese, organic, crumbled

2 large eggs

1 small onion, diced

½ cup of fresh parsley, finely chopped

2 tsp of dried oregano, ground

Preparation:

Combine all ingredients in a large bowl. Mix all well and shape the meatballs using hands.

Take a large baking sheet and place the meatballs. Broil the meatballs on both side until browned. Remove from the oven and let it cool.

Serve meatballs with sour cream, or vegetable salad.

Nutrition information per serving: Kcal: 186, Protein: 14.3g, Carbs: 2.5g, Fats: 14.6g

31.   Italian Egg Drop Soup with Parmesan

Ingredients:

4 cups of chicken broth

2 large eggs

4 tbsp of Parmesan cheese, organic, grated

2 tsp of fresh parsley, finely chopped

¼ tsp of black pepper, ground

Preparation:

Pour the chicken broth into a large pot. Season with pepper and bring it to a boil.

Combine eggs, parsley, and add a pinch of salt and pepper. Whisk well and pour the mixture into the pot. Stir constantly for about 3-4 minutes until eggs start to float.

Serve warm.

Nutrition information per serving: Kcal: 65, Protein: 5.7g, Carbs: 2.1g, Fats: 3.8g

32. Apple Spinach Smoothie

Ingredients:

½ large apple, chopped

2 oz of baby spinach, chopped

2 tbsp of flax seeds

4 tbsp of orange juice

1 tsp of maple syrup

Preparation:

Combine all ingredients in a blender. Blend until smooth and transfer to a serving glass. Add few ice cubes and serve.

Nutrition information per serving: Kcal: 138, Protein: 7.4g, Carbs: 24.5g, Fats: 2.5g

33. Ricotta Pancakes

Ingredients:

2 cups of ricotta cheese, organic crumbled

4 free-range eggs

1 cup of buttermilk, organic

1 tbsp of lemon juice

1 cup of wheat flour

1 tsp of baking powder

½ tsp of salt

1 tbsp of flaxseed oil

Preparation:

Combine flour, baking powder and salt in a mixing bowl. Whisk the eggs, lemon juice, and buttermilk in a separate bowl. Stir in the cheese and toss well. Combine these mixtures and stir well together to get a nice batter.

Preheat the oil in pancake pan over a medium-high temperature. Spoon the batter and spread evenly in the pan.

Cook for 2 minutes, or until bubbly on top and flip over.

Nutrition information per serving: Kcal: 211, Protein: 12.8g, Carbs: 22.2g, Fats: 7.9g

34. Edamame Salad

Ingredients:

1 lb of edamame, shelled

1 red bell pepper, chopped

1 medium-sized red onion, sliced

¼ cup of spring onions, chopped

2 tbsp of fresh basil, finely chopped

For dressing:

5 tbsp of fresh lemon juice

2 tbsp of yellow mustard

2 tbsp of extra-virgin oil

¼ tsp of salt

¼ tsp of black pepper, ground

Preparation:

Combine all dressing ingredients and stir well. Set aside for 10 minutes to allow flavors to meld.

Meanwhile, prepare edamame using package instructions. Drain well and transfer to a salad bowl. Stir in pepper, onion, spring onions, and basil. Drizzle with dressing and toss well. Refrigerate until serving.

Nutrition information per serving: Kcal: 107, Protein: 4.5g, Carbs: 11.2g, Fats: 7.8g

35. Shrimps in Homemade Tomato Sauce

Ingredients:

12 oz of shrimps, deveined and peeled

1 medium-sized tomato, chopped

½ cup of cheddar cheese, organic, shredded

2 garlic cloves, minced

½ cup of heavy cream

2 tbsp of butter

1 tsp of dried oregano, ground

Preparation:

Melt butter in a large frying skillet over a medium-high temperature. Add garlic cloves and stir-fry until translucent.

Add shrimps and pour over tomato sauce. Stir well and reduce temperature to low. Cover with a lid and cook for 20 minutes, or until shrimps are pink.

Add cheese and cream and give it a good stir. Let it cook for 2-3 minutes more and remove from the heat.

You can serve with pasta, rice or vegetables.

Nutrition information per serving: Kcal: 211, Protein: 30.3g, Carbs: 15.6g, Fats: 5.6g

36. Banana Berry Smoothie

Ingredients:

1 medium-sized banana, sliced

1 cup of orange juice

½ cup of fresh raspberries

1 tbsp of chia seeds

Preparation:

Combine banana, raspberries, and orange juice in a blender. Blend until smooth and transfer to a serving glasses. Top with chia seeds. Refrigerate 30 minutes before serving.

Nutrition information per serving: Kcal: 198, Protein: 7.5g, Carbs: 48.3g, Fats: 1.6g

37. Cabbage Rolls

Ingredients:

1 lb of cabbage leaves

1 medium-sized chicken fillet, skinless and boneless, chopped

½ cup of brown rice

5 tbsp of olive oil

1 medium-sized tomato, chopped

½ tsp of Cayenne pepper

1 tsp of fresh parsley, finely chopped

¼ tsp of black pepper, ground

¼ tsp of salt

Preparation:

Combine meat, tomato, rice, and parsley. Add some salt and pepper to taste and stir in 2 tablespoons of oil. Stir well to combine and set aside.

Now, put about 2 tablespoons of this mixture in the centre of a cabbage leaf. Repeat the process with remaining mixture. Roll up nicely and tuck in the ends.

Add remaining oil to a deep pot. If you have any extra cabbage leaves, place them on the bottom. Place the rolls in the and pour enough water to cover all rolls. Sprinkle with cayenne pepper and vegetable seasoning mix. Cover with a lid and reduce the temperature to low. Cook for 1 hour. Remove from the heat and let it cool.

Serve warm.

Nutrition information per serving: Kcal: 202, Protein: 20.5g, Carbs: 21.4g, Fats: 8.8g

38. Kale and Lentil Stew

Ingredients:

3 cups of fresh kale, chopped

1 cup of green lentils

1 cup of white rice

1 cup of homemade tomato paste

1 medium-sized carrot, sliced

1 cup of spring onions, chopped

1 cup of fresh celery, chopped

1 garlic clove, minced

1 tbsp of vegetable oil

1 tbsp of dried oregano, ground

2 tsp of lemon zest

¼ tsp of salt

¼ tsp of black pepper, ground

Preparation:

Heat the oil in a large skillet over a medium-low

temperature. Add celery, carrot, onion, and a tablespoon of water and stir. Cover with a lid and cook for 10 minutes, or until soften. Add garlic and oregano and cook for 2 minutes more. Stir in rice and lentils and bring it to a boil. Cover with a lid and cook for 45 minutes. Now, add kale and cook for another 10 minutes. Remove from the heat and stir in lemon zest, salt, and pepper to taste.

Serve warm.

Nutrition information per serving: Kcal: 291, Protein: 15.2g, Carbs: 62g, Fats: 5.6g

39. Spinach and Strawberry Smoothie

Ingredients:

¼ cup of fresh strawberries, halved

½ cup of fresh spinach, chopped

1 medium-sized banana, chopped

½ cup of Greek yogurt, organic

1 tbsp of chia seeds

Preparation:

Combine all ingredients in a blender except chia seeds. Blend until smooth and transfer to a serving glass. Top with chia seeds and refrigerate 30 minutes before serving.

Nutrition information per serving: Kcal: 196, Protein: 9.8g, Carbs: 45.7g, Fats: 2.7g

40. Cucumbers in Sour Cream

Ingredients:

2 medium-sized cucumbers, peeled and sliced

4 tbsp of sour cream, organic

1 garlic clove, crushed

1tbsp of fresh parsley, finely chopped

1 tbsp of apple cider vinegar

¼ cup of sweet onions, sliced

¼ tsp of paprika, ground

¼ tsp od salt

¼ tsp of black pepper, ground

Preparation:

Combine cucumbers, onions, garlic, salt, and pepper in a large bowl. Pour water enough to cover all. Set it aside for 20 minutes. Transfer all to a colander and drain well. Set aside.

Meanwhile, combine sour cream, parsley, and vinegar in a mixing bowl. Stir well to combine and set aside.

Return the cucumber into a salad bowl and pour over the sour cream mixture.

Give it a good stir and sprinkle with ground paprika for extra flavor.

Serve immediately.

Nutrition information per serving: Kcal: 137, Protein: 2.4g, Carbs: 12.6g, Fats: 7.9g

41. Pumpkin Pie

Ingredients:

15 oz mashed squash

6 fl oz whole milk

½ tsp of cinnamon, ground

½ tsp of nutmeg

½ tsp of salt

3 large eggs

½ cup of granulated sugar

1 pack of pate brisee

Preparation:

Place squash puree in a large bowl.

Now add milk, cinnamon, eggs, nutmeg, salt, and sugar. Whisk together until well incorporated.

Grease and line the baking dish with baking paper. Gently place pate brisee creating the edges with your hands. Pour the squash mixture over and flatten the surface with a spatula.

Place in the oven and bake for 1 hour, or until fully set. Remove from the oven and allow it to stand for at least 30 minutes.

Now gently remove the pie from the baking dish and transfer to a serving platter. Refrigerate overnight and serve.

Nutrition information per serving: Kcal: 188, Protein: 7.5g, Carbs: 51.4g, Fats: 16.2g

JUICE RECIPES

1. Spinach Blackberry Juice

Ingredients:

1 cup fresh spinach, torn

1 cup blackberries

1 cup mango, chunked

3 whole apricots, chopped

1 whole lime, peeled

Preparation:

Rinse the spinach thoroughly under cold running water. Drain and torn into small pieces. Set aside.

Rinse the blackberries using a large colander. Drain and set aside.

Peel the mango and cut into small chunks. Fill the measuring cup and reserve the rest for later. Set aside.

Wash the apricots and cut in half. Remove the pits and chop into small pieces. Set aside.

Peel the lime and cut lengthwise in half. Set aside.

Now, combine spinach, blackberries, mango, apricots, and lime in a juicer. Process until juiced. Transfer to a serving glass and refrigerate for 10 minutes before serving.

Enjoy!

Nutrition information per serving: Kcal: 201, Protein: 11.1g, Carbs: 61.5g, Fats: 2.6g

2. Sweet Apple Ginger Juice

Ingredients:

1 large Granny Smith's apple, cored and chopped

1 small ginger knob, peeled

1 cup celery, chopped

1 cup fresh mint, torn

1 tsp liquid honey

1 oz water

Preparation:

Wash the apple and cut lengthwise in half. Remove the core and cut into bite-sized pieces. Set aside.

Peel the ginger knob and chop into small pieces. Set aside.

Wash the celery and chop into small pieces. Fill the measuring cup and reserve the rest for later.

Rinse the mint thoroughly under cold running water. Drain and torn into small pieces.

Now, combine apple, ginger, celery, and mint in a juicer and process until well juiced. Transfer to a serving glass and stir in the honey and water.

Refrigerate for 15 minutes before serving.

Enjoy!

Nutrition information per serving: Kcal: 121, Protein: 2.6g, Carbs: 35.8g, Fats: 0.8g

3. Pumpkin Pomegranate Juice

Ingredients:

1 cup yellow pumpkin, cubed

1 cup pomegranate seeds

3 whole plums, pitted and chopped

1 medium-sized orange, peeled

¼ tsp ginger, ground

1 oz water

Preparation:

Cut the top of a pumpkin. Cut lengthwise in half and then scrape out the seeds. Cut one large wedge and peel it. Cut into small cubes and fill the measuring cup. Reserve the rest in the refrigerator.

Cut the top of the pomegranate fruit using a sharp paring knife. Slice down to each of the white membranes inside of the fruit. Pop the seeds into a measuring cup and set aside.

Wash the plums and cut into halves. Remove the pits and chop into small pieces. Set aside.

Peel the orange and divide into wedges. Cut each wedge in

half and set aside.

Now, combine pumpkin, pomegranate, plums, and orange in a juicer. Process until juiced. Transfer to a serving glass and stir in the ginger and water.

Refrigerate for 10 minutes before serving.

Enjoy!

Nutrition information per serving: Kcal: 214, Protein: 5.2g, Carbs: 61.8g, Fats: 1.8g

4. Blueberry Grapefruit Juice

Ingredients:

1 cup blueberries

1 whole grapefruit, peeled

1 cup avocado, cubed

1 small Red Delicious apple, cored

¼ tsp vanilla extract

Preparation:

Place the blueberries in a colander. Rinse well under cold running water and drain. Set aside.

Peel the grapefruit and divide into wedges. Cut each wedge in half and set aside.

Peel the avocado and cut lengthwise in half. Remove the pit and cut into small cubes. Fill the measuring cup and reserve the rest in the refrigerator.

Wash the apple and cut lengthwise in half. Remove the core and cut into bite-sized pieces. Set aside.

Now, combine blueberries, grapefruit, avocado, and apple in a juicer and process until juiced. Transfer to a serving glass and stir in the vanilla extract. Refrigerate for 10 minutes before serving.

Nutrition information per serving: Kcal: 436, Protein: 6.4g, Carbs: 69.5g, Fats: 23.2g

5. Orange Carrot Juice

Ingredients:

1 large orange, peeled

1 large carrot, sliced

1 cup butternut squash, cubed

1 whole lemon, peeled

1 cup cucumber, sliced

¼ tsp turmeric, ground

Preparation:

Peel the orange and divide into wedges. Cut each wedge in half and set aside.

Wash and peel the carrot. Cut into thin slices and set aside.

Wash the squash and chop into small cubes. Fill the measuring cup and reserve the rest in the refrigerator. Set aside.

Peel the lemon and cut lengthwise in half. Set aside.

Wash the cucumber and cut into thin slices. Fill the measuring cup and reserve the rest for later.

Now, combine orange, carrot, squash, lemon, and cucumber in a juicer and process until juiced. Transfer to a serving glass and stir in the turmeric.

Add some crushed ice and serve immediately.

Nutrition information per serving: Kcal: 127, Protein: 4.6g, Carbs: 40.7g, Fats: 0.9g

6. Lemon Banana Juice

Ingredients:

1 cup strawberries, chopped

1 whole lemon, peeled

1 large banana, chunked

1 cup pineapple, chunked

1 tbsp fresh mint, finely chopped

Preparation:

Peel the lemon and cut lengthwise in half. Set aside.

Peel the banana and cut into small chunks. Set aside.

Wash the strawberries and remove the stems. Chop into small pieces and fill the measuring cup. Reserve the rest in the refrigerator.

Cut the top of the pineapple using a sharp paring knife. Gently remove all hard skin and slice it into thin slices. Fill the measuring cup and reserve the rest for later.

Now, combine lemon, banana, strawberries, and pineapple in a juicer. Process until juiced. Transfer to a serving glass and stir in the mint.

Add few ice cubes and serve immediately.

Nutrition information per serving: Kcal: 224, Protein: 4.1g, Carbs: 69.4g, Fats: 1.3g

7. Celery Cherry Juice

Ingredients:

1 cup celery, chopped

1 cup cherries, pitted

1 cup watermelon, diced

1 small ginger knob, peeled

1 oz water

¼ tsp cinnamon, ground

Preparation:

Wash the celery and cut into small pieces. Fill the measuring cup and reserve the rest for later. Set aside.

Rinse the cherries under cold running water using a colander. Drain and cut each in half. Remove the pits and set aside.

Cut the watermelon in half. Cut one large wedge and wrap the rest in a plastic foil and refrigerate. Dice the wedge and remove the pits. Fill the measuring cup and set aside.

Peel the ginger knob and cut into small pieces. Set aside.

Now, combine celery, cherries, watermelon, and ginger

knob in a juicer and process until juiced. Transfer to a serving glass and stir in the water and cinnamon. Add some ice and serve immediately.

Nutrition information per serving: Kcal: 143, Protein: 3.4g, Carbs: 40.2g, Fats: 0.7g

8. Pear Lemon Juice

Ingredients:

1 small pear, chopped

1 whole lemon, peeled and halved

1 cup of apricots, pitted and halved

1 tbsp liquid honey

1 small Granny Smith's apple, cored

1 cup fresh mint, torn

Preparation:

Wash the pear and cut in half. Remove the core and cut into small pieces. Set aside.

Peel the lemon and cut lengthwise in half. Set aside.

Wash the apricots and cut each lengthwise in half. Remove the pits and fill the measuring cup. Reserve the rest in the refrigerator for some other juice.

Wash the apple and cut lengthwise in half. Remove the core and chop into bite-sized pieces. Set aside.

Rinse the mint thoroughly under cold running water. Drain and torn into small pieces. Set aside.

Now, combine pear, lemon, apricots, apple, and mint in a juicer and process until well juiced. Transfer to a serving glass and add some ice before serving.

Enjoy!

Nutrition information per serving: Kcal: 217, Protein: 4.9g, Carbs: 68.5g, Fats: 1.5g

9. Melon Apple Juice

Ingredients:

1 large honeydew melon wedge, chopped

1 medium-sized Zestar apple, cored

2 cups blueberries

2 oz coconut water

1 tbsp mint, finely chopped

Preparation:

Cut melon lengthwise in half. Scoop out the seeds and then wash. Cut one large wedge and peel it. Cut into small cubes and set aside.

Wash the apple and cut lengthwise in half. Remove the core and cut into bite-sized pieces. Set aside.

Place the blueberries in a large colander. Rinse well under cold running water and drain. Set aside.

Now, combine honeydew melon, apple, and blueberries in a juicer. Process until juiced.

Transfer to a serving glass and stir in the coconut water, vanilla extract, and mint. Add some crushed ice and serve immediately.

Nutrition information per serving: Kcal: 283, Protein: 3.7g, Carbs: 85.1g, Fats: 1.5g

10. Kiwi Apple Juice

Ingredients:

1 cup celery, chopped

1 whole kiwi, peeled

1 medium-sized Golden Delicious apple, cored

1 medium-sized orange, peeled

1 tbsp liquid honey

¼ tsp ginger, ground

Preparation:

Peel the kiwi and cut lengthwise in half. Set aside.

Wash the apple and cut lengthwise in half. Remove the core and cut into bite-sized pieces. Set aside.

Wash the celery and chop into small pieces. Fill the measuring cup and reserve the rest for later. Set aside.

Peel the orange and divide into wedges. Cut each wedge in half and set aside.

Now, combine kiwi, apple, celery, and orange in a juicer and process until juiced. Transfer to a serving glass and stir in the honey and ginger.

Refrigerate for 15 minutes before serving.

Enjoy!

Nutrition information per serving: Kcal: 172, Protein: 3.5g, Carbs: 51.2g, Fats: 1.1g

11. Apple Nutmeg Juice

Ingredients:

1 large green apple, cored

¼ tsp nutmeg, ground

1 cup cranberries

1 large pear, cored

3 large strawberries, chopped

1 large orange, peeled

2 oz coconut water

Preparation:

Wash the apple and cut in half. Remove the core and cut into bite-sized pieces. Set aside.

Wash the cranberries thoroughly under cold running water. Drain and set aside.

Wash the pear and cut lengthwise in half. Remove the core and cut into bite-sized pieces. Set aside.

Wash the strawberries thoroughly and chop into small pieces. Set aside.

Peel the orange and divide into wedges. Set aside.

Now, combine apple, cranberries, pear, strawberries, orange, and nutmeg in a juicer. Process until well juiced and transfer to serving glasses.

Stir in the water and refrigerate or add some ice before serving.

Nutritional information per serving: Kcal: 158, Protein: 4.7g, Carbs: 47.9g, Fats: 1.1g

12. Peach Gala Juice

Ingredients:

2 large peaches, pitted

1 large Gala apple, cored

1 cup watermelon, cubed

5 fresh cherries, pitted

3 oz coconut water

Preparation:

Wash the peaches and cut in half. Remove the pits and cut into bite-sized pieces. Set aside.

Wash the apple and cut in half. Remove the core and cut into bite-sized pieces. Set aside.

Cut the watermelon lengthwise. For one cup, you will need about one large wedge. Peel and cut into chunks. Remove the seeds and set aside. Reserve the rest of the melon for some other juices.

Wash the cherries and cut in half. Remove the pits and set aside.

Now, process peaches, apple, watermelon, and cherries in

a juicer. Transfer to serving glasses and stir in the coconut water. Add some ice and serve immediately.

Nutritional information per serving: Kcal: 276, Protein: 5.4g, Carbs: 47.6g, Fats: 1.6g

13. Leek Lime Juice

Ingredients:

3 large leeks, chopped

1 large lime, peeled

1 cup cauliflower, chopped

1 large zucchini, chopped

2 oz water

Preparation:

Wash the leeks and cut into small pieces. Set aside.

Peel the lime and cut lengthwise in half. Set aside.

Trim off the outer leaves of cauliflower. Wash it and cut into small pieces. Set aside.

Peel the zucchini and cut in half. Scrape out the seeds and cut into small chunks. Set aside.

Now, combine leeks, lime, cauliflower, and zucchini in a juicer. Process until well juiced and stir in the water. Refrigerate for 10 minutes before serving.

Enjoy!

Nutritional information per serving: Kcal: 241, Protein: 13.2g, Carbs: 64.7g, Fats: 2.6g

14. Apricot Pomegranate Juice

Ingredients:

1 cup of pomegranate seeds

1 large lemon, peeled

1 large apricot, pitted

1 large orange, wedged

1 large carrot, sliced

2 oz coconut water

Preparation:

Cut the top of the pomegranate fruit using a sharp knife. Slice down to each of the white membranes inside of the fruit. Pop the seeds into measuring cup and set aside.

Peel the lemon and cut lengthwise in half. Set aside.

Wash the apricot and cut in half. Remove the pit and cut into small pieces. Set aside.

Peel the orange and divide into wedges. Set aside.

Peel and wash the carrot. Cut into thin slices and set aside.

Now, combine pomegranate seeds, lemon, apricot, orange,

and carrot in a juicer. Process until well juiced and transfer to serving glasses. Stir in the coconut water and add few ice cubes before serving.

Nutritional information per serving: Kcal: 241, Protein: 7.3g, Carbs: 73.9g, Fats: 2.3g

15. Kale Parsley Juice

Ingredients:

1 cup fresh kale, torn

1 cup fresh parsley, torn

2 cups broccoli, trimmed

1 large green apple, chopped

1 cup fresh spinach, torn

2 oz water

Preparation:

Wash the broccoli under cold running water and cut into small pieces. Set aside.

Combine kale, parsley, and spinach in a colander and rinse under cold running water. Drain and torn with hands. Set aside.

Wash the apple and cut in half. Remove the core and cut into bite-sized pieces. Set aside.

Now, combine kale, parsley, broccoli, apple, and spinach in a juicer. Process until well juiced and stir in the water.

Refrigerate for 10 minutes before serving.

Nutritional information per serving: Kcal: 223, Protein: 20.4g, Carbs: 62.1g, Fats: 3.5g

16. Apple Strawberry Juice

Ingredients:

1 large red apple, cored

2 large strawberries, chopped

2 large grapefruits, peeled

1 small ginger knob, peeled

2 oz coconut water

Preparation:

Wash the apple and cut in half. Remove the core and cut into bite-sized pieces. Set aside.

Wash the strawberries and cut into small pieces. Set aside.

Peel the grapefruits and divide into wedges. Set aside.

Peel the ginger knob and set aside.

Now, combine apple, strawberries, grapefruits, and ginger in a juicer. Process until well juiced and transfer to serving glasses. Stir in the coconut water and refrigerate for 20 minutes, or add some ice before serving.

Nutritional information per serving: Kcal: 302, Protein: 4.8g, Carbs: 86.3g, Fats: 1.7g

17. Peach Apple Juice

Ingredients:

2 large peaches, pitted

1 large Red Delicious apple, cored

1 cup strawberries, chopped

1 large lemon, peeled

1 large kiwi, peeled

1 large orange, peeled

2 oz water

Preparation:

Wash the peaches and cut in half. Remove the pits and cut into small pieces. Set aside.

Wash the apple and cut half. Remove the core and cut into bite-sized pieces. Set aside.

Wash the strawberries under cold running water. Remove the green parts and cut into bite-sized pieces. Set aside.

Peel the lemon and kiwi. Cut lengthwise in half and set aside.

Now, combine peaches, apple, strawberries, lemon, and kiwi in a juicer and process until well juiced. Transfer to serving glasses and stir in the water. Add some ice and serve immediately.

Enjoy!

Nutritional information per serving: Kcal: 345, Protein: 7.8g, Carbs: 105g, Fats: 2.3g

18. Raspberry Apricot Juice

Ingredients:

1 cup raspberries

3 large apricots, pitted

1 cup blackberries

1 large Gala apple, cored

3 large carrots, peeled

Preparation:

Combine raspberries and blackberries in a large colander. Rinse under cold running water and slightly drain. Set aside.

Wash the apricots and cut in half. Remove the pits and cut into bite-sized pieces. Set aside.

Wash the apple and cut in half. Remove the core and cut into small pieces.

Wash and peel the carrots. Cut into thin slices and set aside.

Now, combine raspberries, apricots, blackberries, apple, and carrots in a juicer. Process until well juiced and transfer to serving glasses. Stir in the water and refrigerate for 10-15 minutes before serving.

Enjoy!

Nutritional information per serving: Kcal: 301, Protein: 7.6g, Carbs: 97.4g, Fats: 2.9g

19. Kiwi Lime Juice

Ingredients:

3 large kiwis, peeled

1 large lime, peeled

1 large zucchini, seeded

1 cup pomegranate seeds

1 large orange, peeled

Preparation:

Peel the kiwis and lime. Cut lengthwise in half and set aside.

Wash the zucchini and cut in half. Scoop out the seeds using a spoon. Cut into small chunks and set aside.

Cut the top of the pomegranate fruit using a sharp knife. Slice down to each of the white membranes inside of the fruit. Pop the seeds into a measuring cup and set aside.

Peel the orange and divide into wedges. Set aside.

Now, process kiwis, lime, zucchini, pomegranate seeds, and orange in a juicer.

Transfer to a serving glasses and add some ice cubes before serving.

Nutritional information per serving: Kcal: 183, Protein: 8.5g, Carbs: 52.6g, Fats: 1.6g

20. Blueberry Cucumber Juice

Ingredients:

1 cup blueberries

1 large cucumber, sliced

1 cup mango, chopped

1 large Zestar apple, cored

2 oz water

¼ tsp vanilla extract

Preparation:

Place the blueberries in a colander and wash under cold running water. Drain and set aside.

Wash the cucumber and cut into thin slices. Set aside.

Wash the mango and cut into chunks. Fill the measuring cup and reserve the rest for some other juice. Set aside.

Wash the apple and remove the core. Cut into bite-sized pieces and set aside.

Now, combine blueberries, cucumber, mango, and apple in a juicer and process until juiced.

Transfer to serving glasses and stir in the water and vanilla extract. Add some ice before serving and enjoy!

Nutritional information per serving: Kcal: 180, Protein: 5.9g, Carbs: 63.5g, Fats: 1.1g

21. Carrot Watercress Juice

Ingredients:

2 large carrots, sliced

1 cup watercress, torn

1 cup pineapple, chunked

1 large lime, peeled

1 small ginger knob, peeled

2 oz water

Preparation:

Wash and peel the carrots. Cut into thin slices and set aside.

Wash the watercress thoroughly under cold running water. Torn with hands and set aside.

Peel the pineapple and cut into small chunks. Set aside.

Peel the lime and cut lengthwise in half. Set aside.

Peel the ginger root knob and cut into small pieces. Set aside.

Now, combine carrots, watercress, pineapple, lemon, and

ginger in a juicer and process until well juiced.

Transfer to serving glasses and stir in water.

Add some ice and serve.

Nutritional information per serving: Kcal: 135, Protein: 3.3g, Carbs: 40.6g, Fats: 3.3g

22. Lime Celery Juice

Ingredients:

1 large lime, peeled

2 large celery stalks, chopped

2 large grapefruits, peeled

1 large kiwi, peeled

1 cup red leaf lettuce, chopped

2 oz water

Preparation:

Peel the lime and kiwi. Cut in half and set aside.

Wash and chop the celery stalks into small pieces. Set aside.

Peel the grapefruit and divide into wedges. Set aside.

Rinse the lettuce thoroughly under cold running water and roughly chop it. Set aside.

Now, combine lime, celery, grapefruit, kiwi, and lettuce in a juicer and process until well juiced.

Transfer to serving glasses and stir in the water. Serve

immediately.

Nutritional information per serving: Kcal: 233, Protein: 6g, Carbs: 70.7g, Fats: 1.3g

23. Apricot Pomegranate Juice

Ingredients:

2 large apricots, pitted

1 cup pomegranate seeds

2 large oranges, peeled

1 cup green grapes

1 large lemon, peeled

1 small ginger slice, peeled

Preparation:

Wash the apricots and cut in half. Remove the pits and cut into small pieces. Set aside.

Cut the top of the pomegranate fruit using a sharp knife. Slice down to each of the white membranes inside of the fruit. Pop the seeds into a measuring cup and set aside.

Peel the oranges and divide into wedges. Set aside.

Peel the lemon and cut lengthwise in half. Set aside.

Peel the ginger slice and set aside.

Now, combine apricots, pomegranate, oranges, lemon, and

ginger in a juicer. Process until well juiced and transfer to serving glasses. Refrigerate for 10 minutes before serving.

Nutritional information per serving: Kcal: 294, Protein: 7.2g, Carbs: 88.9g, Fats: 2.3g

24. Orange Raspberry Juice

Ingredients:

1 large orange, peeled

1 cup raspberries

2 cups watermelon, chopped

1 large kiwi, peeled

2 oz coconut water

Preparation:

Peel the orange and divide into wedges. Set aside.

Wash the raspberries thoroughly under cold running water. Drain and set aside.

Cut the watermelon lengthwise. For 2 cups, you will need about two large wedges. Peel and cut into chunks. Remove the seeds and set aside. Reserve the rest of the melon for some other juices. Set aside.

Peel the kiwi and cut lengthwise in half. Set aside.

Now, combine watermelon, orange, raspberries, and kiwi in a juicer. Process until juiced and transfer to serving glasses. Stir in the coconut water and refrigerate for 10 minutes before serving.

Nutritional information per serving: Kcal: 232, Protein: 5.8g, Carbs: 71.4g, Fats: 1.8g

25. Sour Apple Mint Juice

Ingredients:

1 large green apple, cored

1 tbsp fresh mint, chopped

1 large papaya, peeled and chopped

1 cup pomegranate seeds

2 oz water

Preparation:

Wash the apple and cut in half. Using a sharp knife, remove the core and cut into bite-sized pieces. Set aside.

Peel the papaya and cut lengthwise in half. Scoop out the black seeds and flesh using a spoon. Cut into small chunks and set aside.

Cut the top of the pomegranate fruit using a sharp knife. Slice down to each of the white membranes inside of the fruit. Pop the seeds into a measuring cup and set aside.

Now, combine apple, mint, papaya, and pomegranate in a juicer. Process until well juiced and transfer to serving glasses. Stir in the water and refrigerate before serving.

Nutritional information per serving: Kcal: 438, Protein: 6.1g, Carbs: 129g, Fats: 3.4g

26. Lime Guava Juice

Ingredients:

1 cup pineapple, chopped

2 large limes, peeled

1 cup guava, chopped

1 large cucumber, sliced

1 tbsp fresh mint, chopped

2 oz water

Preparation:

Peel the limes and cut lengthwise in half. Set aside.

Wash the guava and cut into chunks. Fill the measuring cup and reserve the rest for some other recipe in a refrigerator.

Cut the top of a pineapple and peel it using a sharp knife. Cut into small chunks and fill the measuring cup. Reserve the rest of the pineapple in a refrigerator.

Wash the cucumber and cut into thin slices. Set aside.

Now, combine limes, guava, pineapple, cucumber, and mint in a juicer. Process until well juiced and transfer to serving glasses. Stir in the water and refrigerate for 15 minutes before serving.

Nutritional information per serving: Kcal: 158, Protein: 4.7g, Carbs: 47.9g, Fats: 1.1g

27. Apple Asparagus Juice

Ingredients:

1 large red apple, cored

1 cup asparagus, trimmed

1 cup fresh spinach, torn

1 cup collard greens, torn

1 cup mustard greens, torn

2 oz water

Preparation:

Wash the apple and cut in half. Remove the core and cut into bite-sized pieces. Set aside.

Trim off the woody ends of the asparagus. Rinse well and cut into bite-sized pieces. Set aside.

Combine spinach, collard greens, and mustard greens in a large colander. Wash under cold running water and drain. Torn with hands and set aside.

Now, combine apple, asparagus, spinach, collard greens, and mustard greens in a juicer and process until well juiced. Transfer to serving glasses and stir in the water. Refrigerate for 15 minutes before serving.

Enjoy!

Nutritional information per serving: Kcal: 207, Protein: 16.1g, Carbs: 58.6g, Fats: 2.5g

28. Apple Beet Juice

Ingredients:

1 large Red Delicious apple, cored

1 cup beets, chopped

2 cups raspberries

1 cup fresh mint, torn

1 large lemon, peeled

3 oz water

Preparation:

Wash the apple and cut in half. Remove the core and cut into bite-sized pieces. Set aside.

Wash the beets and trim off the green ends. Cut into small pieces and fill the measuring cup. Reserve the greens for some other juice.

Wash the raspberries under cold running water using a colander. Drain and set aside.

Rinse the mint thoroughly under cold running water and torn with hands. Set aside.

Peel the lemon and cut lengthwise in half. Set aside.

Now, combine apple, beets, raspberries, mint, and lemon in a juicer. Process until well juiced. Stir in the water and refrigerate for 10 minutes before serving.

Enjoy!

Nutritional information per serving: Kcal: 218, Protein: 7.5g, Carbs: 76.4g, Fats: 2.5g

29. Guava Lime Juice

Ingredients:

1 large lime, peeled

2 large oranges, peeled

1 large guava, peeled

1 large cucumber, sliced

2 oz water

1 tsp agave nectar

Preparation:

Peel the lime and cut lengthwise in half. Set aside.

Peel the oranges and divide into wedges. Set aside.

Peel and wash the guava. Cut into small chunks and set aside.

Wash the cucumber and cut into thin slices. Set aside.

Now, combine lime, orange, guava, and cucumber in a juicer and process until juiced.

Transfer to serving glasses and stir in the water and agave nectar. Add some ice and serve immediately.

Nutritional information per serving: Kcal: 210, Protein: 7g, Carbs: 65.7g, Fats: 1.3g

30. Spinach Lemon Juice

Ingredients:

1 cup fresh spinach, chopped

1 large lemon, peeled

1 cup celery, chopped

1 cup fresh mint, chopped

2 oz water

Preparation:

Wash the spinach and mint in a colander. Chop and place in a medium bowl. Set aside.

Peel the lemon and cut lengthwise in half. Set aside.

Wash the celery stalks and chop into small pieces. Fill the measuring cup and set aside.

Now, combine spinach, lemon, celery, and mint in a juicer and process until juiced. Transfer to serving glasses and stir in the water.

Refrigerate for 5 minutes before serving.

Nutritional information per serving: Kcal: 35, Protein: 3.1g, Carbs: 13.2g, Fats: 0.7g

31. Pear Pepper Juice

Ingredients:

1 large pear, cored

1 large red bell pepper, chopped

2 cups beets, chopped

1 large lemon, peeled

1 small ginger root slice, peeled

3 oz water

Preparation:

Wash the pear and cut in half. Remove the core and cut into bite-sized pieces. Set aside.

Wash the bell pepper and cut in half. Remove the seeds and cut into small pieces. Set aside.

Wash the beets and trim off the green ends. Cut into small pieces and fill the measuring cup. Reserve the greens for some other juice. Set aside.

Peel the lemon and cut lengthwise in half. Set aside.

Peel the ginger slice and cut in half. Set aside.

Now, combine pear, bell pepper, beets, lemon, and ginger in a juicer. Process until well juiced and transfer to serving glasses.

Stir in the water and add some ice before serving.

Enjoy!

Nutritional information per serving: Kcal: 239, Protein: 7.5g, Carbs: 76.7g, Fats: 1.4g

32. Apple Cinnamon Juice

Ingredients:

1 large Granny Smith's apple, cored

¼ tsp cinnamon, ground

2 cups pumpkin, cubed

1 large cucumber, sliced

1 cup Swiss chard, torn

2 oz water

Preparation:

Wash the apple and cut in half. Remove the core and cut into bite-sized pieces. Set aside.

Peel the pumpkin and cut in half. Scoop out the seeds using a spoon. Cut one large wedge and peel it. Cut into small cubes and fill the measuring cup. Reserve the rest for some other juice.

Wash the cucumber and cut into thin slices. Set aside.

Wash the Swiss chard thoroughly under cold running water. Drain and torn with hands. Set aside.

Now, combine apple, pumpkin, cucumber, and Swiss

chards in a juicer. Process until well juiced and stir in the water and nutmeg.

Refrigerate for 10 minutes before serving.

Nutritional information per serving: Kcal: 196, Protein: 5.8g, Carbs: 55.4g, Fats: 1.1g

33. Pomegranate Plum Juice

Ingredients:

1 cup pomegranate seeds

4 large plums, pitted

1 large red bell pepper, chopped

1 cup cranberries

1 large Gala apple, cored

Preparation:

Cut the top of the pomegranate fruit using a sharp knife. Slice down to each of the white membranes inside of the fruit. Pop the seeds into a measuring cup and set aside.

Wash the plums and cut in half. Remove the pits and cut into bite-sized pieces. Set aside.

Wash the bell pepper and cut lengthwise in half. Remove the seeds and cut into small pieces. Set aside.

Wash the cranberries thoroughly and drain. Set aside.

Wash the apple and cut in half. Remove the core and cut into bite-sized pieces. Set aside.

Now, combine pomegranate, plums, cranberries, and

apple in a juicer. Process until well juiced and add some ice before serving.

Enjoy!

Nutritional information per serving: Kcal: 277, Protein: 6g, Carbs: 83g, Fats: 1.4g

34. Blackberry Cucumber Juice

Ingredients:

1 cup blackberries

1 large cucumber, sliced

5 large plums, pitted

1 cup green cabbage, chopped

2 oz water

Preparation:

Rinse the blackberries under cold running water using a colander. Slightly drain and set aside.

Wash the cucumber and cut into thin slices. Set aside.

Wash the plums and cut in half. Remove the pits and cut into quarters. Set aside.

Wash the cabbage thoroughly under cold running water. Drain and roughly chop it. Set aside.

Now, combine blackberries, cucumber, plums, and cabbage in a juicer and process until juice. Transfer to serving glasses and stir in the water. Refrigerate for 10 minutes before serving.

Nutritional information per serving: Kcal: 221, Protein: 7.5g, Carbs: 69.1g, Fats: 2.1g

35. Lemon Lime Juice

Ingredients:

1 large lemon, peeled

1 large lime, peeled

1 large artichoke, chopped

1 medium-sized zucchini, chopped

1 cup fresh mint, chopped

1 cup purple cabbage, chopped

2 oz water

Preparation:

Peel the lemon and lime. Cut lengthwise in half and set aside.

Trim off the outer leaves of the artichoke. Wash it and cut into bite-sized pieces. Set aside.

Peel the zucchini and cut lengthwise in half. Scoop out the seeds and peel it. Cut into bite-sized pieces and set aside.

Combine mint and cabbage in a colander. Rinse thoroughly under cold running water and roughly chop it. Set aside.

Now, combine lemon, lime, artichoke, zucchini, basil, and cabbage in a juicer. Process until well juiced and stir in the water.

Refrigerate for 15 minutes before serving.

Enjoy!

Nutritional information per serving: Kcal: 104, Protein: 10.4g, Carbs: 38.1g, Fats: 1.3g

36. Green Salty Juice

Ingredients:

1 cup watercress, torn

1 cup collard greens, torn

1 cup asparagus, trimmed

1 green bell pepper, chopped

1 large cucumber, sliced

2 oz water

¼ tsp salt

Preparation:

Combine watercress and collard greens in a colander. Wash thoroughly under cold running water and torn with hands. Set aside.

Wash the asparagus and trim off the woody ends. Cut into bite-sized pieces and fill the measuring cup. Reserve the rest for some other juice.

Wash the bell pepper and lengthwise in half. Remove the seeds and chop into small pieces. Set aside.

Wash the cucumber and cut into thin slices. Set aside.

Now, combine watercress, collard greens, asparagus, bell pepper, and cucumber in a juicer and process until well juiced. Transfer to serving glasses and stir in the salt and water. Refrigerate for 10-15 minutes before serving.

Nutritional information per serving: Kcal: 86, Protein: 8.2g, Carbs: 26.1g, Fats: 1g

37. Asparagus Lemon Juice

Ingredients:

1 cup fresh asparagus, trimmed and chopped

1 whole lemon, peeled

1 cup pomegranate seeds

1 tbsp liquid honey

1 oz water

Preparation:

Wash the asparagus and trim off the woody ends. Cut into bite-sized pieces and set aside.

Peel the lemon and cut into quarters. Set aside.

Cut the top of the pomegranate fruit using a sharp paring knife. Slice down to each of the white membranes inside of the fruit. Pop the seeds into a measuring cup and set aside.

Now, combine asparagus, lemon, and pomegranate seeds in a juicer and process until well juiced. Transfer to a serving glass and stir in the honey and water.

Add some ice and enjoy!

Nutritional information per serving: Kcal: 145, Protein: 5.1g, Carbs: 26.8g, Fats: 1.3g

38. Blueberry Lime Juice

Ingredients:

2 cups blueberries

1 whole lime, peeled

1 cup watermelon, cubed

1 cup fresh mint, torn

¼ tsp cayenne pepper, ground

1 oz water

Preparation:

Place the blueberries in a large colander. Rinse well under cold running water and set aside.

Peel the lime and cut lengthwise in half. Set aside.

Cut one large watermelon wedge. Using a sharp paring knife, peel and cut into small cubes. Remove the seeds and set aside.

Rinse the basil and roughly torn it with hands. Set aside.

Now, combine blueberries, lime, watermelon, and basil in a juicer. Process until juiced. Transfer to a serving glass and stir in the cayenne pepper and water.

Refrigerate for 5 minutes before serving.

Nutritional information per serving: Kcal: 198, Protein: 4.1g, Carbs: 58.7g, Fats: 1.4g

39. Mango Mint Juice

Ingredients:

1 cup mango, cut into chunks

1 cup fresh mint, roughly chopped

1 whole grapefruit, peeled

1 large banana, peeled

2 large strawberries, chopped

Preparation:

Peel the mango and cut into small chunks. Fill the measuring cup and reserve the rest in the refrigerator. Set aside.

Rinse the mint roughly and torn with hands. Set aside.

Peel the grapefruit and divide into wedges. Cut each wedge in half and set aside.

Peel the banana and cut into small pieces. Set aside.

Wash the strawberries and remove the stems. Cut into bite-sized pieces and set aside.

Now, combine mango, mint, grapefruit, banana, and strawberries in a juicer and process until juiced. Transfer to a serving glass and add some ice cubes before serving.

Enjoy!

Nutritional information per serving: Kcal: 301, Protein: 5.9g, Carbs: 88.5g, Fats: 1.7g

40. Beet Orange Juice

Ingredients:

1 whole beet, sliced

1 small mandarin orange, wedged

1 cup pineapple, chunked

2 tbsp coconut water

¼ tsp ginger, ground

Preparation:

Wash and trim off the beet. Cut into small slices and set aside.

Peel the orange and divide into wedges. Cut each wedge in half and set aside.

Cut the top of a pineapple and peel it using a sharp paring knife. Cut into small chunks and fill the measuring cup. Reserve the rest of the pineapple in a refrigerator.

Now, combine beet, orange, and pineapple in a juicer and process until juiced. Transfer to a serving glass and stir in the coconut water and ginger.

Add some crushed ice and serve immediately.

Nutritional information per serving: Kcal: 135, Protein: 3.1g, Carbs: 40.7g, Fats: 0.5g

41. Kale Mint Juice

Ingredients:

1 cup celery, chopped

1 cup fresh kale, torn

1 cup fresh mint, torn

1 whole lime, peeled

1 small Granny Smith's apple, cored

Preparation:

Combine kale and mint in a large colander. Wash thoroughly under cold running water. Slightly drain and torn with hands. Set aside.

Wash the celery and chop into small pieces. Fill the measuring cup and set aside.

Peel the lime and cut into small pieces. Set aside.

Wash the apple and cut in half. Remove the core and cut into bite-sized pieces. Set aside.

Now, combine kale, mint, celery, lime, and apple in a juicer and process until juiced. Transfer to a serving glass and add some ice before serving.

Enjoy!

Nutritional information per serving: Kcal: 121, Protein: 5.3g, Carbs: 35.8g, Fats: 1.3g

42. Celery Zestar Juice

Ingredients:

2 medium-sized celery stalk, chopped

1 small Zestar apple, cored

1 cup fresh kale, chopped

1 cup Romaine lettuce, shredded

Preparation:

Wash the celery stalks and cut into bite-sized pieces. Set aside.

Wash the apple and cut in half. Remove the core and cut into small pieces. Set aside.

Wash the kale thoroughly under cold running water. Slightly drain and chop it into small pieces. Set aside.

Wash the lettuce leaves and shred it. Fill the measuring cup and reserve the rest for later.

Now, combine celery, apple, kale, and lettuce in a juicer and process until juiced. Transfer to a serving glass and add some ice before serving.

Enjoy!

Nutritional information per serving: Kcal: 103, Protein: 4.6g, Carbs: 29.4g, Fats: 1.2g

43. Green Ginger Juice

Ingredients:

1 cup collard greens, chopped

2 cups Swiss chard, chopped

1 cup fresh kale, chopped

1 whole lemon, peeled

1 cup cucumber, sliced

¼ tsp ginger, ground

Preparation:

Combine collard greens, Swiss chard, and kale in a large colander. Rinse thoroughly under cold running water. Slightly drain and roughly chop all. Set aside.

Peel the lemon and cut lengthwise in half. Set aside.

Wash the cucumber and cut into thin slices. Fill the measuring cup and reserve the rest in the refrigerator. Set aside.

Now, combine Swiss chard, kale, collard greens, lemon, and cucumber in a juicer. Process until juiced.

Transfer to a serving glass and stir in the ginger.

Serve cold.

Nutritional information per serving: Kcal: 57, Protein: 6.3g, Carbs: 17.8g, Fats: 1.2g

44. Broccoli Cucumber Juice

Ingredients:

1 cup of broccoli, chopped

1 cup of cucumber, sliced

1 large red bell pepper, chopped

1 large celery stalk, chopped

¼ tsp of ginger, ground

Preparation:

Wash the broccoli and trim off the outer wilted layers. Cut into small pieces and set aside.

Wash the cucumber and cut into thin slices. Fill the measuring cup and reserve the rest in the refrigerator.

Wash the pepper and cut in half. Remove the seeds and stem. Cut into thin slices and set aside.

Wash the celery stalk and cut into small pieces. Set aside.

Now, combine pepper, broccoli, cucumber, and celery in a juicer and process until well juiced. Transfer to a serving glass and stir in the ginger.

Refrigerate for 10 minutes before serving.

Nutritional information per serving: Kcal: 71, Protein: 4.9g, Carbs: 19.7g, Fats: 1g

45. Brussels Sprout Carrot Juice

Ingredients:

1 cup of Brussels sprouts, trimmed

1 large carrot, sliced

1 large artichoke, peeled and chopped

1 cup of fresh celery, chopped

1 cup of turnip greens, chopped

1 large green apple, cored

½ tsp of turmeric, ground

2 oz of water

Preparation:

Trim off the outer leaves of the Brussels sprouts and wash them thoroughly. Cut in half and set aside.

Wash the carrot and cut into thin slices. Set aside. Using a sharp knife, trim off the outer leaves of the artichoke. Cut into small pieces and set aside.

Wash the celery and chop it into bite-sized pieces. Set aside.

Wash the apple and cut in half. Remove the core and cut into bite-sized pieces. Set aside.

Wash the turnip greens thoroughly and torn with hands. Set aside.

Now, combine Brussels sprouts, carrot, artichoke, celery, turnip greens, and apple in a juicer. Process until well juiced and transfer to serving glasses. Stir in the turmeric and water. Add some ice before serving.

Nutritional information per serving: Kcal: 205, Protein: 11.3g, Carbs: 66.7g, Fats: 1.4g

46. Butternut Squash Parsnip Juice

Ingredients:

3 large red bell peppers, chopped

1 cup of butternut squash, cubed

1 cup of parsnip, sliced

1 tbsp of fresh parsley, chopped

¼ tsp salt

2 oz of water

Preparation:

Peel the butternut squash and remove the seeds using a spoon. Cut into small cubes and fill the measuring cup. Reserve the rest of the squash for some other recipe. Wrap in a plastic foil and refrigerate.

Wash the parsnip and peel it. Cut into thin slices and set aside.

Wash the red bell peppers and cut lengthwise in half. Remove the seeds and chop into small pieces.

Now, combine butternut squash, parsnip, bell peppers, and parsley in a juicer. Process until well juiced and transfer to serving glasses. Stir in the water and salt. Add some ice and serve immediately.

Nutritional information per serving: Kcal: 238, Protein: 7.9g, Carbs: 70.2g, Fats: 2.1g

47. Apple Mango Juice

Ingredients:

1 medium-sized apple, cored

1 cup mango, chunked

1 cup of pomegranate seeds

1 small ginger slice

¼ tsp cinnamon, ground

1 oz water

Preparation:

Wash the apple and cut lengthwise in half. Remove the core and cut into small pieces. Set aside.

Peel the mango and cut into chunks. Fill the measuring cup and reserve the rest in the refrigerator. Set aside.

Cut the top of the pomegranate fruit using a sharp paring knife. Slice down to each of the white membranes inside of the fruit. Pop the seeds into a measuring cup and set aside.

Peel the ginger slice and chop into small pieces. Set aside.

Now, combine apple, mango, pomegranate seeds, and ginger in a juicer and process until juiced. Transfer to a serving glass and stir in the cinnamon and water.

Refrigerate for 10 minutes before serving.

Nutrition information per serving: Kcal: 227, Protein: 3.6g, Carbs: 64.1g, Fats: 1.9g

48. Carrot Watercress Juice

Ingredients:

1 large carrot, sliced

1 cup watercress, torn

1 cup pumpkin, cubed

1 small Golden Delicious apple, cored and chopped

1 whole lemon, peeled

Preparation:

Wash and peel the carrot. Cut into thin slices and set aside.

Rinse the watercress thoroughly under cold running water. Drain and torn into small pieces. Set aside.

Cut the top of a pumpkin. Cut lengthwise in half and then scrape out the seeds. Cut one large wedge and peel it. Cut into small cubes and fill the measuring cup. Reserve the rest in the refrigerator.

Wash the apple and cut lengthwise in half. Remove the core and cut into bite-sized pieces. Set aside.

Peel the lemon and cut lengthwise in half. Set aside.

Now, combine carrot, watercress, pumpkin, apple, and

lemon in a juicer and process until juiced. Transfer to a serving glass and add some ice before serving.

Enjoy!

Nutrition information per serving: Kcal: 126, Protein: 3.6g, Carbs: 37.8g, Fats: 0.7g

49. Pineapple Spinach Juice

Ingredients:

1 cup pineapple, chunked

1 cup spinach, chopped

1 cup cherries, pitted

1 whole lemon, peeled

¼ tsp cinnamon, ground

1 oz water

Preparation:

Using a sharp paring knife, cut the top of the pineapple. Gently remove all hard skin and slice it into thin slices. Fill the measuring cup and reserve the rest for later.

Rinse the spinach thoroughly under cold running water. Drain and chop into small pieces. Set aside.

Place the cherries in a medium colander. Rinse well under cold running water and remove the stems, if any. Cut each in half and remove the pits. Fill the measuring cup and reserve the rest in the refrigerator.

Peel the lemon and cut lengthwise in half. Set aside.

Now, combine pineapple, spinach, cherries, and lemon in a juicer and process until juiced. Transfer to a serving glass and stir in the water.

Add some crushed ice and serve immediately.

Nutrition information per serving: Kcal: 196, Protein: 9.2g, Carbs: 59.3g, Fats: 1.5g

50. Orange Apple Juice

Ingredients:

1 cup papaya, chopped

1 large orange, peeled

1 small Granny Smith's apple, cored

1 cup fresh mint, torn

1 tbsp fresh basil, torn

Preparation:

Peel the orange and divide into wedges. Cut each wedge in half and set aside.

Wash the apple and cut in half. Remove the core and cut into bite-sized pieces. Set aside.

Wash and peel the papaya. Cut lengthwise in half and scoop out the seeds. Cut into bite-sized pieces and fill the measuring cup. Reserve the rest in the refrigerator.

Rinse the mint and basil thoroughly under cold running water. Drain and torn into small pieces. Set aside.

Now, combine orange, apple, papaya, mint, and basil in a juicer and process until juiced. Transfer to a serving glass and add some ice.

Serve immediately.

Nutrition information per serving: Kcal: 199, Protein: 4.1g, Carbs: 60.1g, Fats: 1.1g

51. Parsnip Carrot Juice

Ingredients:

1 cup parsnip, sliced

1 large carrot, sliced

1 cup cauliflower, chopped

1 cup fennel, trimmed and chopped

1 whole lime, peeled

Preparation:

Wash and peel the parsnip. Cut into thin slices and fill the measuring cup. Reserve the rest for later.

Wash and peel the carrot. Cut into thin slices and set aside.

Wash the cauliflower and trim off the outer leaves. Cut into small pieces and fill the measuring cup. Reserve the rest for later.

Trim off the fennel stalks and outer wilted layers. Wash and chop the fennel into bite-sized pieces. Fill the measuring cup and reserve the rest for later. Set aside.

Peel the lime and cut lengthwise in half. Set aside.

Now, combine parsnip, carrot, cauliflower, fennel, and lime

in a juicer. Process until well juiced.

Transfer to a serving glass and refrigerate for 10 minutes before serving.

Add some turmeric or ginger for some extra taste. However, it's optional.

Nutrition information per serving: Kcal: 141, Protein: 5.6g, Carbs: 46.2g, Fats: 1.1g

ADDITIONAL TITLES FROM THIS AUTHOR

70 Effective Meal Recipes to Prevent and Solve Being Overweight: Burn Fat Fast by Using Proper Dieting and Smart Nutrition

By

Joe Correa CSN

48 Acne Solving Meal Recipes: The Fast and Natural Path to Fixing Your Acne Problems in Less Than 10 Days!

By

Joe Correa CSN

41 Alzheimer's Preventing Meal Recipes: Reduce or Eliminate Your Alzheimer's Condition in 30 Days or Less!

By

Joe Correa CSN

70 Effective Breast Cancer Meal Recipes: Prevent and Fight Breast Cancer with Smart Nutrition and Powerful Foods

By

Joe Correa CSN

www.ingramcontent.com/pod-product-compliance
Lightning Source LLC
Chambersburg PA
CBHW052032070526
44584CB00016B/2003